*To SELAH,*
*BE A PROUD MICHIGANDER!*

# EDDY ELK AND MANDY MOOSE

## BY RUSSELL SLATER
### ILLUSTRATED BY LAURA GORDON

Peninsulam Publishing

Publishing stories Made in Michigan
www.peninsulampublishing.com
Printed in the USA

*For Eli.*

This book belongs to: seVan

EDDY ELK AND MANDY MOOSE

HAVE STEPPED OUT OF THE FLAG, THEY'RE ON THE LOOSE!

ALL ACROSS MICHIGAN, THE TWO LIKE TO ROAM

WHAT WILL THEY SEE BEFORE RETURNING HOME?

LOWER YOUR VOICE, PLEASE DON'T SHOUT

YOU'LL SCARE AWAY OUR STATE FISH, THE ELUSIVE BROOK TROUT

STATE FISH: BROOK TROUT

A FACT SO INTERESTING, I *MUST* PASS IT ON

MICHIGAN'S STATE FOSSIL IS THE MASTODON

MICHIGA

HISTORY MU

MASTODON

STATE FOSSIL: MASTODON

THE FRUIT IS SWEET, THE SMELL IS AWESOME

OUR OFFICIAL STATE FLOWER IS THE APPLE BLOSSOM

STATE FLOWER: APPLE BLOSSOM

AND HERE'S *ANOTHER* THAT CAN'T BE MISSED

IT'S MICHIGAN'S WILDFLOWER, THE DWARF LAKE IRIS

STATE WILDFLOWER: DWARF LAKE IRIS

PRETTY AS A PICTURE, THEY ALWAYS MAKE ME SMILE

THE COLORFUL PAINTED TURTLES ARE MICHIGAN'S STATE REPTILE

STATE REPTILE: PAINTED TURTLE

OUT HERE IN THE WOODS, THERE'S NOTHING TO FEAR

LOOK!  IT'S OUR FRIEND, THE WHITETAIL DEER

STATE MAMMAL: WHITETAIL DEER

WHEN CHRISTMAS NEARS, THERE'S NO SIGHT AS FINE

AS MICHIGAN'S STATE TREE, THE GORGEOUS WHITE PINE

**STATE TREE: WHITE PINE**

WE LOVE MiCHiGAN, THERE'S SO MUCH TO SEE!

DON'T FORGET OUR STATE STONE, FOUND NEAR PETOSKEY

STATE STONE: PETOSKEY STONE

ONE OF THE NEATEST ANiMALS WE'VE SEEN OR HEARD

IS THE RED BREAST ROBiN, MiCHiGAN'S STATE BiRD

STATE BIRD: RED BREAST ROBIN

A PECULIAR ROCK, THE ODDEST EVER KNOWN

IS OUR STATE GEM, THE ISLE ROYALE GREENSTONE

STATE GEM: CHLORASTROLITE (ISLE ROYALE GREENSTONE)

IT'S NOT ORDINARY DIRT ON WHICH WE STAND

IT'S OUR STATE SOIL, CALLED KALKASKA SAND

STATE SOiL: KALKASKA SAND

ON OUR WAY HOME, NOTHING'S QUITE AS SUPER

AS A HELPING HAND FROM A FRIENDLY STATE TROOPER

WE MICHIGANDERS ARE ALWAYS ADVENTURE-BOUND

SO IF YOU SEEK A PLEASANT PENINSULA, TAKE A LOOK AROUND

## ABOUT THE AUTHOR

Russell Slater is a writer from western Michigan. His work has been published in the (Wayland) Penasee Globe, Allegan County News, Engraver's Journal, Flavor 616 Magazine, and the Volunteer: Civil Air Patrol Magazine. He lives in a rural community with his wife and son.


Contact the author:

Russell@peninsulampublishing.com

## About the Illustrator

Laura Gordon is a graphic designer and artist living in sunny, beachside California. Owner of thebookcovermachine.com, she has designed hundreds of book covers for authors all around the world. When she isn't creating something new, Laura can be found enjoying the beach, a good book, or doting on her feline children, Moo and Charlie.

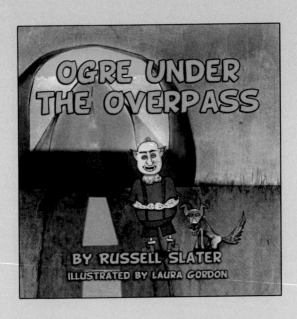